*To those who choose
a better journey*

Design work by Jordan Stockill
ISBN 978-1-8380251-0-6

Journey Stage	Page
Introduction	5
No. 1 route: The Now Bus	7
Current Journey	7
The Big Question, where my bus is heading, journey satisfaction	8
The thoughts of fellow travellers	13
No. 2 route: The Yesterday Bus	15
Past journey	15
What I'm proud of in each ten-year period of my life	16
When I've been most happy	17
What has shaped me?	18
At the interchange	19
Planning the new journey; journey checklist	19
Purpose, values and talents	19
My life journey planner: what I want to achieve in life	25

Timetabling and witnessing 28

No. 3 route: The Future Bus 31

How I'll get there 31

The life goals approach – breaking the journey into smaller, manageable stages 31

Monitoring progress, reviewing goals, celebrating achievements and milestones, adding new goals 35

Mindset and qualities for the journey 36

My support network along the way 55

We're off 56

Imagine life as three bus journeys: a past,
a present, a future

You choose the one for the latest journey

And now you're aboard, is it heading to where you truly want to go?

The Three Journeys System

The three bus journeys life coaching map

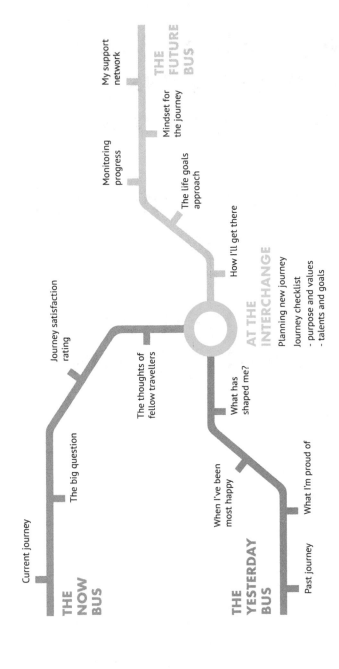

THE NOW BUS

Current journey

The big question

Journey satisfaction rating

The thoughts of fellow travellers

AT THE INTERCHANGE

How I'll get there

Planning new journey
Journey checklist
- purpose and values
- talents and goals

What has shaped me?

THE YESTERDAY BUS

When I've been most happy

What I'm proud of

Past journey

THE FUTURE BUS

My support network

Mindset for the journey

Monitoring progress

The life goals approach

INTRODUCTION

Are you on the right bus?
A bus journey is an ideal metaphor for life. There are many landmarks and stopping-off points along the way and there are likely to be traffic build ups and one or two detours. You're moving but are you on the right bus? Is it taking you to where you need to be? And how's the scenery looking? If you're constantly sensing that the journey isn't working out the way you wanted, get off at the interchange, consult the network map and timetable and plan the one you're meant to be on.Every significant journey needs planning which makes it remarkable that some people spend more time planning a holiday than they do their life. They react to the highs and lows rather than look ahead to where their bus is taking them and what the road might be like further on.

This book – your life bus map and guide
This life coaching book provides a simple means of planning your new life journey. It involves three buses and an interchange. You'll gauge where you are now, where you want to be and how you'll get there. You'll also look at where you've come from as this has some bearing on the route you choose. This appraisal of your journey to date and the future you want requires commitment and there'll be some soul searching.

A word about life coaching
Life coaching is about using the right questions and techniques to unlock potential and working towards realising it. It must not be confused with mentoring, counselling or medical intervention. Anyone needing help because they are experiencing challenging mental issues should seek the services of an expert in this field and not a life coach.

It's about the journey
Avoid the thought that happiness is the destination otherwise you'll spend a lifetime catching all the buses and missing out on the wonderful views from the vehicle window. Enjoy the journey and the personal growth that comes from following the process of achieving your life goals.

Let's begin.

No. 1
ROUTE: THE NOW BUS

Current journey
Your current bus is one of many you might have caught. Some take you on pleasant excursions like trips to the beach but they're just for the day and there are others that take you some distance, but the scenery is less than inspiring. Does the grid below give you any ideas about your own journey?

High		

Distance and Effort	Limited Stop Intercity	Pullman Journey of a Lifetime
	Shuttlebus	Day Tripper
	Enjoying the view	

Low   **High**

Life bus journey model. Straughan, 2019

The big question
What's bothering you? What has prompted you to seek out a life coaching solution? Is there a nagging feeling that you're capable of achieving so much more but success is always on the horizon? Spend a few minutes working out what answers you're after.

The wheels of the bus go round and round...
A well-established life coaching tool for understanding our current position is the Wheel of Life which was originally developed by Paul J. Meyer, founder of Success Motivation® Institute Inc. It provides a quick diagnostic of what's going well and what isn't. There have been various interpretations with different labels but, generally, they provide a satisfaction reading of a snapshot in time.

Here's how the Wheel of Life works.
Draw a circle and divide it into the following eight sections:

- Career
- Health
- Finances
- Home and neighbourhood
- Relationships/loved ones
- Social
- Hobbies and pastimes
- Personal growth

Now write a zero at the centre and the number '10' at the part of the outer ring at the top of each segment.

See the template and completed examples on the next page.

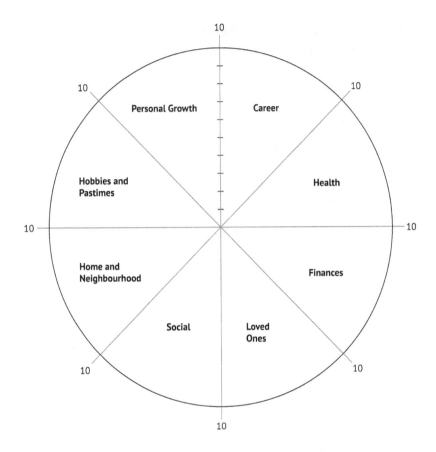

Take zero as **dissatisfied** and 10 as **completely satisfied** and draw a line across each segment to note how satisfied you are at this point in life.

Here's an example of a Wheel of Life completed:

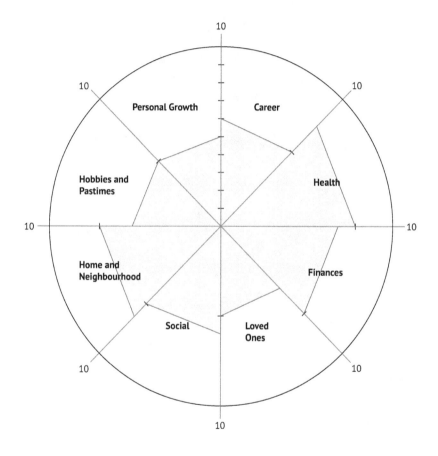

Now back to your Wheel of Life:

1. What does it tell you?
2. How many areas of your life need addressing?
3. How are they influencing other segments?
4. What is the prize for improving them and what is the price for allowing everything to remain the same?

Keep this wheel until you gauge your contentment score in the months to come.

Your fellow travellers

There are other travellers on your life journey. These include loved ones and friends, colleagues, neighbours and society to name a few. What will these travellers – your life stakeholders – say about you when the journey is over? Imagine the journey has reached its final stop and each of them has contributed to your eulogy. What words will they use to describe you and the role you played in their lives? How will they rate your journey?

Use the grid on the next page to note your answers.

My Fellow Travellers	What they'll say about me

No.2

ROUTE: THE YESTERDAY BUS — WHERE YOU'VE COME FROM

Past journey
Just as any journey preparation requires a clear understanding of where we are now, it also requires us to know where we've come from. The travels of the past have influenced who we've become.

What I'm proud of to date
As we said earlier, life coaching is about identifying potential and taking steps to realise it. Using the grid on the next page, look back over your life to date and consider what you have achieved in each ten-year period. Some achievements will spring to mind quickly but others you have temporarily forgotten. List them all — from learning to read or ride a bicycle to getting your first place to live independently or achieving some academic or career success. Everything is relative; what might seem a minor achievement will have been a big deal for

that stage of your life. And how you made that achievement possible will give an insight into your character and approach to life.

Age	Achievements
0-10	
11-20	
21-30	
31-40	
41-50	
51-60	
Etc.	

BUS STOP

When were you at your happiest?

Has there been a time when you've been at your happiest? What did it feel like, look like and sound like? Was it enjoyable because you were positively immersed in what you were doing? Use the grid below to record the experience(s).

Time(s) in life when truly happy	I was (where?) and doing (what exactly?)	Factors that made this time so special

What has shaped me?
Or this question can be put as: what have I allowed to shape me?

We can choose whether to define ourselves or allow people and events to define us. It's fine to take on positive attributes of those who have been influential in our life, but we don't have to take on the negative ones, too.

We can choose our response to something that disappoints us instead of a reaction we might regret. As the saying goes: *Once the toothpaste is out the tube, you can't get it back in.*

Think about the challenges you have faced and how you responded to them. Identify the benefits of choosing a response rather than reacting. When something happens that disappoints, press the pause button and think carefully.

AT THE INTERCHANGE

Planning the new journey.
You're at the interchange because you've decided to change buses. You're consulting the route map and timetable because these will help you find the right bus and departure time.

Journey checklist: purpose, values, skills and talents
At this journey planning stage, you'll identify what you want from life but before you do, ensure you're clear about your purpose, your values and your talents. Your bus journey route needs to encompass these and we'll begin with purpose.

What's your purpose?
Purpose gives meaning to life. Some people are driven by a desire to help others or to leave a positive legacy. Your purpose lies at the heart of where four roads on your journey meet. This is according to the principles of Ikigai, the Japanese philosophy of having a reason for being. In other words, the reason why we get out of bed. These four roads pose questions about what you're good at, how you can earn a living, what you love doing and what society or the world needs. Answer the questions they pose on the next page to find your purpose.

What I love doing

_____

_____

_____

_____

What I'm good at

_____

_____

_____

_____

How I can earn a living

_____

_____

_____

What society/the World needs

_____

_____

_____

_____

You can retire from a job, but don't ever retire from making extremely meaningful contributions in life.

Stephen Covey, businessman, educator and author of *The 7 Habits of Highly Effective People*.

My values

Values influence our behaviour and attitude and provide a framework for the way we live. They are borne out of important beliefs or ideals about what we believe is good and bad and are usually shared by our broader culture.

We project a personal brand to others and our values are at the heart of it. Imagine you're a business, what values drive it? It's likely you'll choose the values that are core to how you live your life.

List your values

My Values	Why and what they say about me	How they influence my behaviour and attitude

My skills and talents

Your purpose will see you making the best possible use of your skills and talents. Take a few moments to list them. You might be surprised by how many there are.

Skills and Talents	Strengths	Useful to develop to help fulfil my purpose

Miller's Law states that the average person can hold seven plus or minus two objects in their short-term memory.

Turning hopes and dreams into goals: my life journey planner

We hold so many hopes and dreams in our minds that we're rarely aware of how many there are at any one time. They come to the fore or return to the recesses of our minds at intervals. It's difficult to hold several thoughts in our mind at once.

In fact, **seven** is the magic number according to Miller's Law which states that the average person can hold seven plus or minus two objects in their short-term memory. This means that people can hold a range of between five and nine objects in their minds at one time. The law is named after Harvard cognitive psychologist George A Miller.

The flow of hopes and dreams

The next part of the process requires at least half an hour and some skilled facilitating. The aim is to get each hope and dream from your head and onto paper. If they remain in your head, they're only hopes and dreams. We're going to turn these thoughts into the goals – the key landmarks – of your new bus journey.

Grab a set of Post-it Notes and stick two on a big sheet of brown paper or a plain wall to create two columns. The first Post-it Note says **Personal** and the other says **Professional.**

Now start the flow of desires big and small. Write each one on its own Post it. These might range from wanting to take a loved one somewhere special for being supportive or learning a new language or skill to becoming a renowned expert in your field. And what about that book you were always going to read but never found the time? Put that on your list.

See the example on the next page

Example: what I want to achieve in life

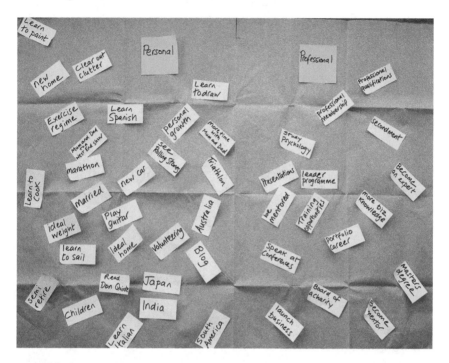

Experience from coaching hundreds of clients tells us that thirty to forty Post-it Notes are the average. It's amazing to see what you've been storing over the years. It's important to capture everything.

When you've completed the list, stand back and make observations. Are they a complete list of what you want from life and what you can contribute to life?

Time for a timetable

Great. Now that you've identified everything (at this point) that you want to achieve, let's agree when you'll make it all happen. Organise your lifetime goals as follows:

- Short term (for example, within the next two years)
- Medium term (within the next five years)
- Long term (six years and beyond)

See the following timescale example with the three darker Post it Notes indicating each timescale on the left and the goals arranged in rows to the right of them.

Example: timetabling my goals

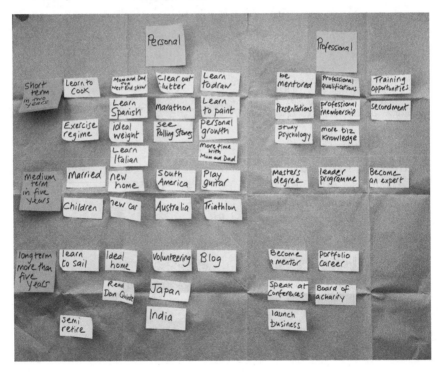

This is your journey plan which you'll review regularly. Admittedly, on a practical point, you're unlikely to find carrying with you a giant sheet of brown paper (or a wall) and a load of Post-its convenient so write your timetabled goals down again in the format of the journey life planner that follows on the next page. And keep it close by. Some people even fold their planner small and carry it in their purse or wallet so it's always at hand. You'll be reviewing your goals regularly, crossing off the ones you've achieved and adding news ones along the journey. Studies show that the action of writing is much better than typing for reinforcing something in your mind. And avoid simply taking a photograph to record what you've created unless it's a back-up.

Witnessing your life journey plan
You'll notice on the grid that there are areas for signing and witnessing. This is crucial for motivation and support. You're now going to sign and date this life planner and ask someone you trust to witness and date it. Choose someone who believes in your potential and who will be constructive, realistic and supportive.

The life planner gives us a broad timescale within which to achieve our goals. When we set out on the next bus – the No. 3 future bus route – we'll drill down into the actions to make them become a reality with specific sub timescales.

My life journey planner		
	Personal	Professional
Short term (eg within two years)		
Medium term (within five years)		
Long term (eg six years and beyond)		
	Signed	**Date**
	Signed (witness)	**Date**

No.3

ROUTE: THE FUTURE BUS — HOW WE'LL GET THERE

Now, it's getting exciting. So far, we've identified everything (at this point) that we want to achieve short term, medium term and long term. It's now time to make the journey manageable.

Breaking the bus journey into smaller stages
There are most likely some big goals because this is your life journey we're planning, and second, it's about your immense potential. To avoid being overwhelmed by the size of it all, we're going to break each journey goal into a set of sub goals with their own milestones. And we turn to the widely popular acronym of SMART to help us achieve our objectives.

Smart action planning

- **Specific** – you must have a clear idea of what it is you need to do. Being vague will be like trying to jump onto a moving bus.
- **Measurable** – you must be able to demonstrate that you're making progress towards the goal. This needs to be quantifiable with a clear achievement

deadline. If you can't measure it, why bother?

- **Achievable** –breaking goals down into more manageable tasks makes them easier to achieve. Check that you have the resources you need.
- **Relevant** – make sure that each goal is in line with your beliefs and values. Is it what you want?
- **Timely** – set timescales to achieve the goal by. Avoid over optimism when the goal will be achieved and avoid setting deadlines that are too far away as the gap will fill with distractions.

See the example on the next page.

Example: overarching goal to secure a role in my work's Human Resources department within two years. Sub goal is to develop my learning so I'm ready for any opportunities that arise.

SMART steps	What the step requires	Details
Specific	State what I'll achieve	Develop my HR learning
Measurable	How I'll measure progress towards my goal The difference it will make	• CIPD qualifications • Current workplace feedback • Boost confidence and knowledge
Achievable	Breakdown of tasks	• Study professional certificates • Ask for work shadowing opportunity • Set up meetings with each of the HR team to learn more about their roles • Read professional magazines and blogs • Check jobs boards

Relevant	This is what I want. It's in line with my purpose and beliefs	• I want to help people improve their performance in work, assist them with employee programmes etc
Timely	I will achieve the goal/sub goal by	• Within 24 months

Monitoring progress, reviewing goals, celebrating achievements, adding new goals
Have you heard the saying: *Today is the first day of the rest of your life*? The point being made is that this is all the time we have so make the most of it. We're going to get the most from our journey by ensuring we're organised, productive and making progress.

Write your daily tasks as soon as you get up each morning or before you go to bed the night before. List everything you're going to achieve that day. At the end of the day, review what you've achieved. If you want to be super organised, you might consider bullet journaling, a system developed by Ryder Carroll. He created his successful way to be focused and productive after being diagnosed with learning challenges in his younger years. There are countless advocates who describe his system as a game changer. And celebrate your successes. This is important because it reinforces what your achievements mean. Is it time to revise or add any new goals?

Mindset for the journey
A strong mindset requires strong doses of:

Gratitude – draw your grati-tuna
It's a major challenge to operate with high-octane optimism every minute of our bus journey especially if despondency creeps in and sabotages our efforts.

However, being thankful for what we have is a powerful weapon. It's difficult to be negative when we're feeling grateful. Psychologists have found that gratitude is good for us because it boosts our happiness and builds physical and psychological wellbeing.

To give some structure to the gratitude process, we're going to draw a grati-tuna – the bone structure of a tuna fish with each thing we're thankful for and each fond memory attached to a bone. The bones joining the spine from the top form an arc while the underside has a number of short bones roughly the same length which appear in front of another arc of bones.

Using the template and completed example that follow, here's how it works:

Step 1: Upper bones – note everything for which you're grateful right now in life. Note: avoid writing down any items that might be deemed as materialistic.

Step 2: Underside short bones – note the small items around you that evoke warm feelings such as a pebble from your favourite beach holiday, a certificate of achievement, an old concert ticket or a table place name from a celebration.

Step 3: Underside arc bones – note the top fond memories that would keep you going if you were shipwrecked on a desert island.

Take a look at the template and the completed example.

What I'm thankful
for right now

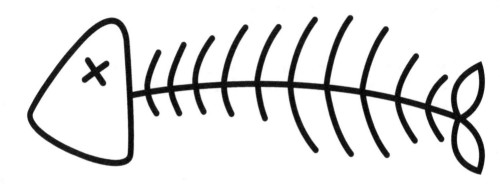

Small objects that give
me a warm feeling

Memories to keep me
strong on a desert island

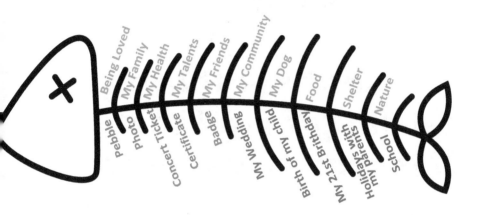

What I'm thankful for right now

Small objects that give me a warm feeling

Memories to keep me strong on a desert island

Each time you draw a grati-tuna, you'll notice that it moves you to a more positive state. It might be a surprise to see how much there is to appreciate. And if you have all this to be grateful for at this stage in life, think how much more there might be as you progress on life's new bus journey.

Some people grumble that roses have thorns; I am grateful that thorns have roses.

Taken from *Letters Written from My Garden*, Alphonse Karr, nineteenth century French journalist and author.

Spend a few minutes reflecting on your attitude to gratitude. Do you find fault or do you find something for which to be thankful?

Mindfulness: much of what we have discussed is about reaching our potential and this requires us to   think about what we can create in the days, months and years ahead. However, we must avoid rushing headlong into the future. We must focus on enjoying the process and being in touch with what's going   on inside us and outside of us.

When we're caught up in our actions and thoughts, it's easy to lose track of what's happening around us and how we feel. Mindfulness is a useful practice because it teaches us to focus on being in the moment. According to Professor Mark Williams, former director of the Oxford Mindfulness Centre, mindfulness is knowing what's going on inside and outside ourselves, moment by moment, waking up to the sights, sounds, smells and tastes. This equips us to enjoy the world around us and understand ourselves better.

When eating, use all your senses to enjoy the experience. When reading a paperback, be aware of the feel and sound as you turn the pages, or, if you're scrolling through this manual on an electronic device, be aware of the sensation. And how does your seating position feel? What's the texture of the chair like and how do your feet feel on the floor?

Meditation is a practice that's associated with mindfulness and isn't confined to sitting still. It's possible to walk and meditate as well. The aim is to get ourselves into a calm and relaxed state, focused on breathing and filtering out distractions.

Studies show that mindfulness can help us develop and embrace good habits while reducing or eliminating bad ones. It can improve our focus and ability to deal with setbacks and help protect our immune system. It also allows us to process feelings and thoughts calmly and accurately without making judgement.

There are countless resources on how to practise mindfulness but, here in the UK, the NHS website is a good place to start.

Motivation: it's the fuel that keeps us going. It's the psychological process that gets us to do what we do and comes in the form of external and internal influences.

- External influences: for instance, from other people or events, tend to have a temporary impact but are essential for helping get out of danger.

- Internal influences: these include personal drive and determination and are more likely to lead to longer-lasting impact. Internal influences have two main drivers: avoiding pain and pursuing pleasure.

Persistence: the resolve to keep going, the staying power that believes something is worth pursuing. This type of tenacity helped Liverpool football club claim one of the most astonishing victories in European competition history. The club has won several trophies over the decades but the most memorable was when it faced six-time European champions AC Milan in what has been dubbed the "miracle of Istanbul." Playing at the Atatürk Stadium in Istanbul in May 2005, Liverpool were 3–0 down at half-time but scored three goals in a six-minute spell in the second half to level. Extra time followed with no goals, so it came down to a penalty shoot-out during which Liverpool goalkeeper Jerzy Dudek saved an Andriy Shevchenko penalty giving the UK team the trophy. The club was able to keep the trophy as it was its fifth European Cup victory, so a new trophy was commissioned.

In his half-time talk, captain Steven Gerrard told the players that he was a Liverpool kid who didn't want to see his club humiliated. He said if Liverpool scored in the first 15 minutes of the second half, they would win the game. Gerrard scored the first goal.

Positivity: because it enables you to see your potential and motivates you. It's been documented that patients in hospital who focus on how well they are progressing recover more quickly than those who worry about what's wrong.

Realism: for anticipating barriers well in advance. This enables you to have prepared to navigate them much better.

Resilience: we all suffer knocks and setbacks, but these can make us stronger depending on our mindset. Resilience is the art of bouncing back instead of wallowing in self-pity. It's about accepting that the road isn't always easy. There are many entrepreneurs whose businesses have gone bust and sports people who have been injured or sidelined but who have had the resilience to come back stronger and able to deal with future challenges.

Tackling procrastination – the enemy of motivation
Calling procrastination laziness is too simplistic. It's a much more complex issue and the subject of a great deal of research. Sometimes not being able to address negative emotions or low self-esteem are behind the problem. However, there are ways of tackling it such as:

Benefits
Earlier, we talked about the prize for action and the price of inaction. Think how some hard work now will make life so much easier in the long run. Imagine enjoying the fruits of your labours. To maintain this focus write down how different you'll feel in a short table as follows:

My goal:	
The prize for being proactive and making it happen	**The price of failing to take action**

Here's an example of how it might look in the case of deciding to achieve better work-life balance.

My goals: better work-life balance	
The prize for being proactive and making it happen	**The price of failing to take action**
Feeling healthier and more alert	Stressed and tired
More energy and time to devote to the neglected areas of my life	Missing out on time with family, hobbies and pastimes
Sleeping better	Troubled sleep

Get a witness
The main reason for requiring someone to witness and sign your goals plan is because it encourages you to make a commitment. You're unlikely to want to lose face by failing to act on your plan. Telling other people will motivate you to do what you say you'll do.

Preparation
Minimise the amount of effort required on the day by getting everything prepared in advance. If you've stated your intention to go to the gym, have your gear ready the night before.

Seeing yourself as a noun as part of your identity
We know that verbs are those doing words; the ones that roll up their sleeves and get stuck into whatever needs doing but did you know that nouns can be more influential when linked to our identity? This is what a California-based study of voting intentions in the 2008 US presidential elections found (Bryan, Walton, Rodgers and Dweck. More participants in the study who were addressed as *voters* went to the ballot box than those who were simply asked about *voting*. So, it's better to say I'm a *marathon runner* and live out my identity rather than *I do marathons* if we want the motivation to put the running shoes on after a day at   work.

Self-talk
It's been estimated that from an early age, we're subjected to twice as many negative statements as positive ones. The danger here is that, once we leave our childhood behind,

we absorb this thinking as the norm and repeat the cycle. Start by flipping negative thoughts and comments into positive ones.

The reason for this is because your subconscious is listening to everything you say and acting on it however damaging or preposterous the self-talk. Start listening to your vocabulary and phrases – are they helpful or harmful? Self-esteem influences our choice of words. Consider what differentiates those with high self-esteem from those with low self-esteem and the type of language they use in the following examples.

Low self esteem	High self esteem
I'm an idiot	Well, that didn't go according to plan. What can I do differently?
I'm rubbish at statistics	There's an opportunity for me to become better at understanding statistics.
What on earth was I thinking?	I'll be better prepared next time

Phew! That was lucky!	That was good
Thanks for the praise but I didn't do anything special	Thanks. It's great to get such feedback. So pleased that what I did has helped.

Don't think of a pink elephant!

During my times in business and industry, I attended personal effectiveness courses where this was discussed. At the time, the pink elephant seemed an amusing diversion. It was only after becoming a life coach that I understood the power of the message. Learning how to rephrase instructions positively to your subconscious can be a game-changer. It's important to understand what the subconscious processes and what it ignores.

Industrial pioneers like Henry Ford, the father of modern assembly were masters in writing their own dialogues. Their self-talk was programmed to look at the possible rather than the impossible. Ford, who is reported to have gone bust five times before finally succeeding, is credited with saying: If you think you can, you can. And if you think you can't, you're right. In other words, if we integrate what we tell ourselves into our belief system, we determine the outcome good or bad.

Speculative words and phrases
Rooting out words like could, should, would, could have, should have and would have is a good move. Such conditional tenses are speculative. Replace them with can, shall and will.

And rein your use of the word 'try.' It lacks belief in a positive outcome. If you use it because of a fear of failure, the following motivational views will help:

- There is no such thing as failure, simply outcomes of actions
- Failure is one step towards success.

Commercial electric lightbulb pioneer Thomas Edison said he found thousands of ways that didn't work before finding the one that did.

Self-confidence and body language
Much of what we communicate is done so via body language. Adopting more open, friendly and confident styles conveys to others that we are winners and it makes us feel good. You might be aware of the saying *fake it till you make it*. It works. Walk with your head high and your chin raised, and the rest of your body will follow. And so, will your feelings.

Take the pink elephant statement to tusk
As stated earlier, many of us have heard the instruction not to think of a pink elephant and, hey presto, no matter how hard we block it out, a pink elephant comes to mind; not just a pink elephant but a giant one at that. Sometimes we'll make statements we think are putting us on the right road when in fact they're sending us back on ourselves especially when they include the words 'no' and 'not' which some experts say the subconscious is unable to process. These statements need flipping, for example:

Negatively directed focus	Positively directed focus
I'm not going to eat cream cakes from now on	I'm eating healthy foods from this point
I'm not going to be late again	I'll arrive on time
Smoking isn't good for me	I'll only do what's good for my lungs

You're the average of the five people you spend most time with.

Jim Rohn — described as one of the leading business philosophers.

See the section My Support Network and spend a few minutes considering the impact others have on your thinking.

My support network

Sixteenth century English poet John Donne wrote that we're not islands entire of ourselves. In other words, there are other people who make up our world who influence us. Jim Rohn, described as one of the greatest business philosophers, follows this theme with his observation that we're the average of the five people we spend most time with. Taking Rohn's observation, it can be useful to carry out an influence audit of those we choose to have close to us personally and professionally. When we discuss our intentions, our hopes and our fears with our fellow passengers on life's bus journey, we want constructive challenge and moral support. While it's true that we must avoid blind devotion which can be damaging, we must also give a wide berth to the fears or misaligned thinking of others that might sabotage our efforts consciously or unconsciously.

Carrying out an audit might bring uncomfortable truths to light. The aim is to gauge how healthy these relationships are for our personal growth and wellbeing. So, which ones do we cultivate and which might we cull? If culling the negative ones sounds drastic, then at least consider reducing the amount of time spent with those whose views are unhelpful.

We're off

At last, you've caught a new bus. It's clean and shiny and looks like it's rolled off the production line. You have your travelling companions and the commitment to see out the journey. You'll regularly check in with those who believe in you to ensure that progress is good and you'll discover so much about yourself as you reach the many milestones. You'll cross off goals from your list and add new ones. You're clear in purpose and know whose lives you enrich. And you're enjoying the journey.

So pleased you bought a ticket

CPSIA information can be obtained
at www.ICGtesting.com
Printed in the USA
LVHW081938250520
656560LV00003B/24

9 781838 025106